BE CREATIVE

Customise Your Clothes

Anna Claybourne

W
FRANKLIN WATTS
LONDON•SYDNEY

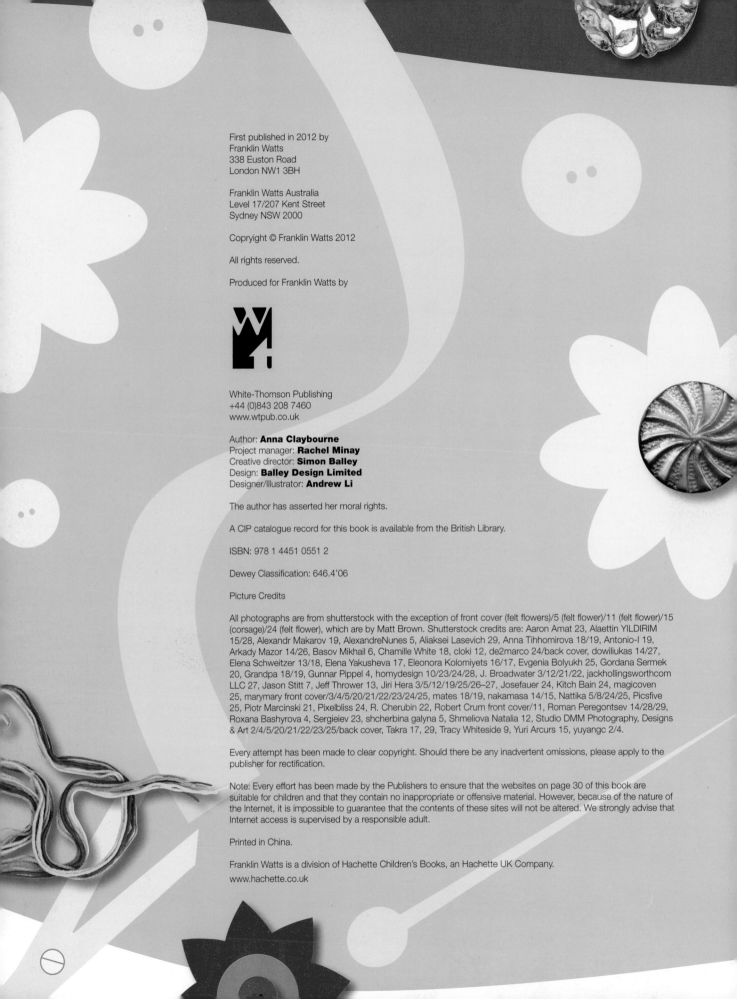

First published in 2012 by
Franklin Watts
338 Euston Road
London NW1 3BH

Franklin Watts Australia
Level 17/207 Kent Street
Sydney NSW 2000

Produced for Franklin Watts by

White-Thomson Publishing
+44 (0)843 208 7460
www.wtpub.co.uk

Author: **Anna Claybourne**
Project manager: **Rachel Minay**
Creative director: **Simon Balley**
Design: **Balley Design Limited**
Designer/Illustrator: **Andrew Li**

The author has asserted her moral rights.

A CIP catalogue record for this book is available from the British Library.

ISBN: 978 1 4451 0551 2

Dewey Classification: 646.4'06

Printed in China.

Franklin Watts is a division of Hachette Children's Books, an Hachette UK Company.
www.hachette.co.uk

Contents

Words in **bold** are in the glossary on page 31.

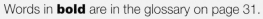

Creative thinking

Craft has never been so cool! Everyone's designing, making and **customising**. This book shows you how to turn old clothes into something new, and stamp your own style on them.

Get the gear!

Besides using your own old clothes, look in charity shops and jumble sales for fabulous finds. You may have basic sewing items, such as pins, needles, thread and scissors, at home. If not, you can buy them at craft shops or department stores – along with a range of fabrics and **haberdashery**, such as beads, buttons, ribbons and trimmings.

Why do it?

When you customise your clothes, you can express yourself and have things just the way you want them. You save money too, and learn skills that could even lead to a crafty career.

Safety

Remember to keep strings, cords and sharp things like pins, needles and scissors away from small children.

Tip!

If you have a sewing machine and know how it works, you can use it for some of the projects in this book.

Tip!
Look for a shoebox, food container or toolbox to store all your sewing stuff and your **'stash'** in. That's the crafty name for your collection of favourite fabrics, beads and trimmings.

You're the boss
Remember, you don't need to follow all the instructions in this book exactly. If you like, just use the methods and ideas to come up with your own creations.

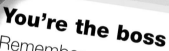

It's green as well!
Customising is a great way to recycle. You can jazz up things you're bored with, rework clothes that are worn out or don't fit, and use up fabric scraps and other odds and ends. Just remember to check with whoever buys your clothes before slicing up or decorating half of your wardrobe!

T-shirt picture

With this simple method, you can sew a picture onto a T-shirt, vest, hoodie or whatever you like.
It works best on plain, flat fabrics.

Get the gear!

- T-shirt or other **garment**
- Pencil and paper
- Needle with a large eye
- **Embroidery** thread (also called stranded cotton) in a bright colour
- Scissors
- **Sewing chalk**

1 First, sketch your design on paper. Start with something easy, such as a star, a heart, a piece of fruit or a bug.

2 Copy the design lightly onto the T-shirt using a pencil or sewing chalk.

3 Cut a piece of embroidery thread about 50cm long. Thread the needle (lick the end of the thread to make it easier) and tie a knot at the long end.

6

4 Push the needle through from the inside of the T-shirt at the start of your design. Then, holding one hand inside the T-shirt, sew neatly along the line, using **backstitch** (see box below).

Tip!
Use backstitch when you need to make a strong seam or **hem**.

5 When you've finished, sew through to the inside of the T-shirt again, tie a knot and snip the thread.

How to do backstitch

1 Push the needle tip in and out of the fabric, making a small stitch.
2 Go back to where the thread disappears into the fabric and push the needle in.
3 Do another stitch, coming out a bit further along.
4 Do the same with each stitch, going back to fill in the space left by the stitch before.

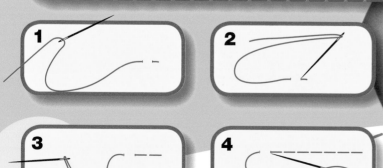

Ribbons and trimmings

Glam up a boring top, jeans, hoodie or anything you like by sewing on a ribbon, decorative trimming or lace edging.

Get the gear!

- Clothes you want to customise
- Needles, pins and sewing thread
- Scissors
- Ribbons and trimmings

1 To add a ribbon trim to a V-neck top, you'll need about 1m of ribbon. Starting at the back of your top, lay the ribbon along the edge of the fabric, and pin it in place. Work all the way around to where you started.

2 To go around a V-neck point, fold the ribbon over itself like this.

3 To finish, trim the ribbon to a little longer than you need, fold the end over and pin it on top of the other end.

How to do overstitch

1 Thread your needle and knot the end of the thread.

2 Poke the needle tip under the edge you want to sew, push it through both fabrics, and pull towards you.

3 Move the needle along slightly and do the same again. Keep stitching like this all the way around, then knot the thread and snip off.

Tip!
Use overstitch to sew along the edge of fabric. It is also useful when fabric needs to stretch.

Now use **overstitch** (see box above) to sew the ribbon to the top. Sew both the outer and inner edges of the ribbon, and also where it folds over itself. Remove the pins.

4

More ideas
Using the same method, you can sew ribbon around a hat, around the hood of your hoodie, along the top of a pocket, or around a skirt hem. Or sew it around the edge of the inside of your jean legs then turn them up!

Felt flowers

Attach these funk-tastic flowers to a cardie, a dress or your favourite woolly hat.

Get the gear!

- 2 or 3 squares of thick felt
- Selection of buttons
- Pencil, scissors and a needle
- Extra-strong thread

1

To make one flower, draw a flower outline on one piece of felt. On a contrasting colour, draw a smaller circle that will fit inside the flower.

2

Cut out both pieces and lay the circle on top of the petals. Choose a button and pop it right in the middle.

Tip!
You could draw around a coin or a button to help you make a perfect circle.

3

Cut some thread, thread your needle and tie a knot in the end of the thread.

4

How to sew on a button

Thread a needle and knot the end of the thread. Sew in from the back or inside of your fabric or garment. Stick the needle through one hole in the button, back through the other hole and through the fabric again. Sew in and out through both holes about 10 times. Knot and snip off the thread at the back of the fabric.

Holding the three parts in position, sew them together through the holes on the button (see box above).

5

Now it's ready to attach! Sew it where you want it to go – or fix with a safety pin if you want it to be detachable.

Jazz up your jeans

Add some decoration to your denim jeans to turn them into something really special.

Get the gear!

- Needles, thread, scissors, pencil and paper
- Embroidery thread
- Buttons, **sequins** or beads (check first the holes are big enough for a needle)
- Sewing chalk

Pocket picture

1

Use the method on pages 6–7 to sew a picture or **slogan** (or both!) onto a jeans pocket. Bright or light colours will stand out best.

2

For extra impact, sew around the shape a few times in different colours. You can also add buttons, beads or sequins.

Tip!

Sewing onto a pocket or leg can be a bit awkward. Scrunch up the edge of the pocket or the end of the leg, so you can hold one hand at the back of the fabric while you sew.

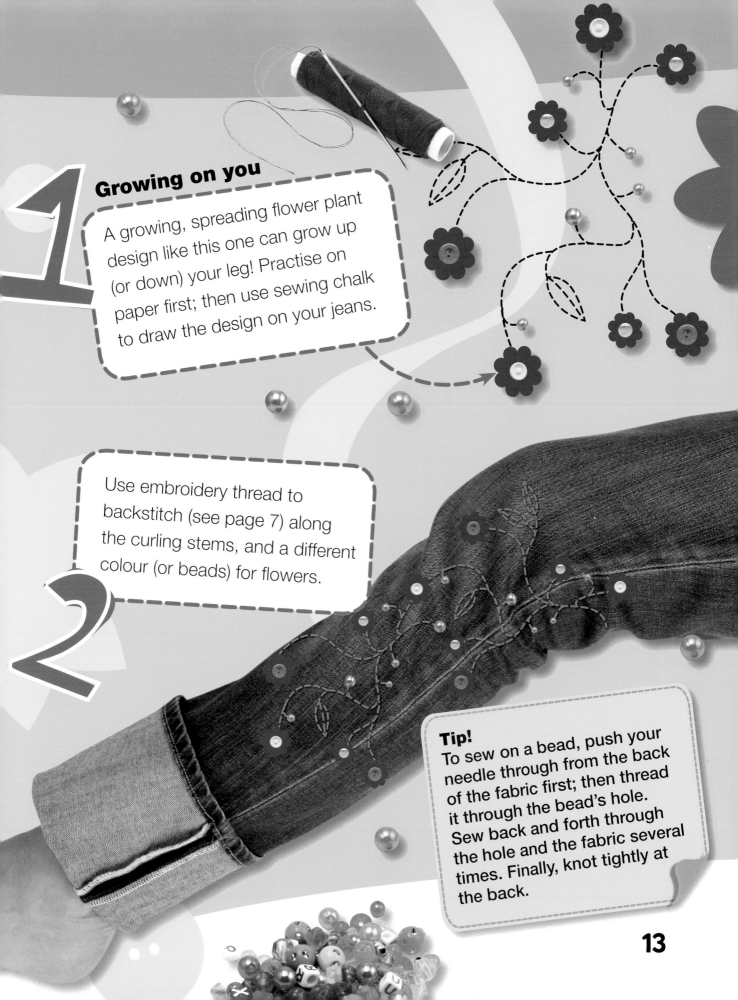

Growing on you

1

A growing, spreading flower plant design like this one can grow up (or down) your leg! Practise on paper first; then use sewing chalk to draw the design on your jeans.

2

Use embroidery thread to backstitch (see page 7) along the curling stems, and a different colour (or beads) for flowers.

Tip!
To sew on a bead, push your needle through from the back of the fabric first; then thread it through the bead's hole. Sew back and forth through the hole and the fabric several times. Finally, knot tightly at the back.

Chic corsage

A **corsage** is a small bouquet of flowers worn on your clothes. These fabric flowers look great on a belt, hat or dress and are easy to make. Wear one to make a bold statement or put a few together for a bouquet.

Tip!
Experiment with different fabrics. Plain, silky material makes a good rose, or use printed cotton for a funky or folky flower.

Get the gear!

- Strip of fabric, about 10cm wide and 50cm long
- Needle, scissors and thread

1 First, fold the strip of fabric in half lengthways.

2 Thread the needle and knot one end of the thread. Sew the edges of the strip together, about 1cm in, using **running stitch** (see box below) with quite large stitches (about 1cm long).

How to do running stitch
Running stitch is a very simple stitch where you simply sew in and out of the fabric in a straight line. It is most useful for sewing thick fabrics, **gathering** fabrics or to make a decorative stitch.

3 When you've sewn to the end, gently pull the thread and push the fabric along it, so that it gathers (crinkles up) a little. Then knot the thread to keep it gathered, and snip off the rest.

4 Now roll the strip up on the stitched edge. Let the other side open out loosely as you roll.

5 Sew a few stitches through the rolled-up side to fix it, and flatten out the 'petals'. Now sew the flower wherever you want it, or attach it with a safety pin.

Trousers to shorts

When the knees on your jeans get a big hole in them, turn them into shorts instead!

Get the gear!

- Old jeans
- Tape measure or ruler
- Scissors, pins, needles and extra-strong thread

1 Put the jeans on and decide how long you want your shorts to be. Mark the length with a few pins (don't stab yourself!) and take the jeans off.

2 Lay the jeans down carefully folded in two (so the legs line up). Cut the legs off 5cm below the pins. Cut across both legs at the same time to make sure they're an equal length.

16

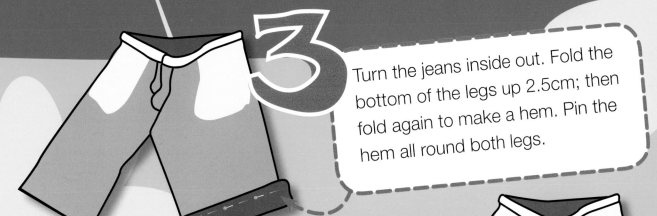

3 Turn the jeans inside out. Fold the bottom of the legs up 2.5cm; then fold again to make a hem. Pin the hem all round both legs.

Tip!
Ironing the hem flat will give a sharper edge and make it easier to sew. You should ask an adult to help you.

4 Thread a needle and knot the thread, then sew around the edge of each hem using backstitch (see page 7). Remove the pins, then turn your shorts the right way out – they're done!

Tip!
Try using contrasting thread – jeans often have yellow or orange stitching. Or decorate your shorts using **appliqué** (see page 26) or bead art (see page 20).

Cool cuffs

Do you ever get chilly wrists? Make your sleeves longer and cosier by adding some snuggly knitted cuffs. This looks good on a coat or denim jacket, and it's a great way to reuse holey old socks and sweaters.

Get the gear!

- Garment you want to add cuffs to, e.g. coat or jacket
- Old sweater or pair of socks
- Scissors and tape measure or ruler
- Pins, needles and extra-strong thread

1 Lay your item of clothing with the sleeves pressed flat. You'll need an old sweater that has sleeves the same width, or a pair of worn-out woolly socks that are the right size.

2 Cut off the sleeves or the tops of the socks to the length you want, plus about 2cm. A good length for a cuff is about 6–8cm.

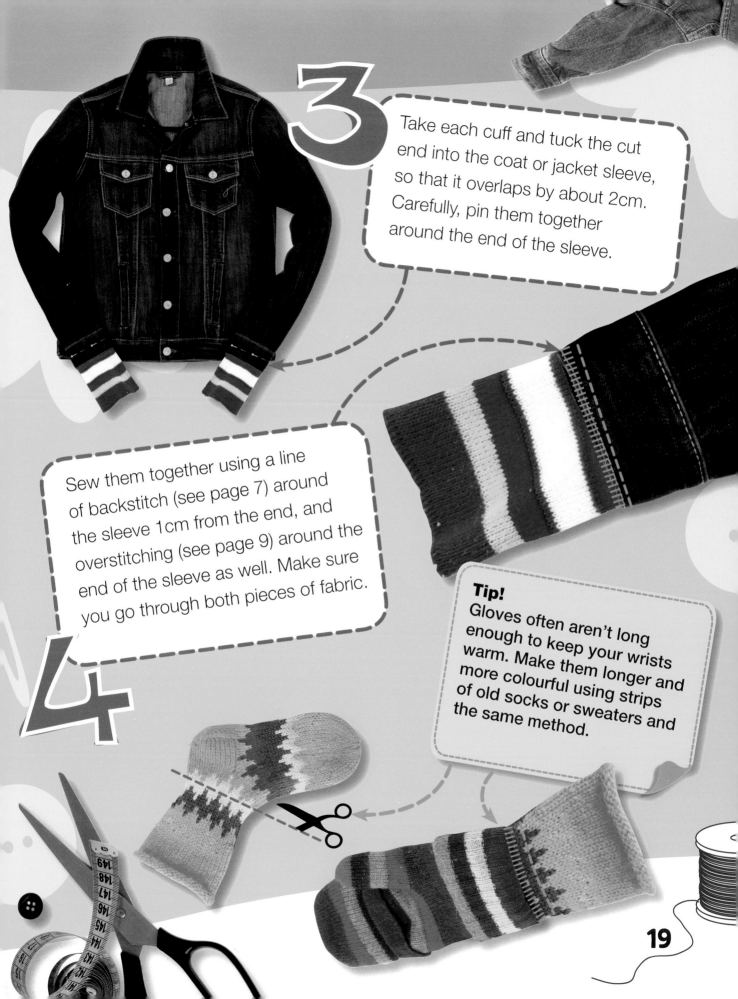

3

Take each cuff and tuck the cut end into the coat or jacket sleeve, so that it overlaps by about 2cm. Carefully, pin them together around the end of the sleeve.

Sew them together using a line of backstitch (see page 7) around the sleeve 1cm from the end, and overstitching (see page 9) around the end of the sleeve as well. Make sure you go through both pieces of fabric.

4

Tip!
Gloves often aren't long enough to keep your wrists warm. Make them longer and more colourful using strips of old socks or sweaters and the same method.

19

Beads and buttons

Just think of all the billions of beads and buttons in the world! They come in all shapes, colours and designs, and are perfect for customising clothes.

Get the gear!

- Beads and buttons (check first the holes are big enough for a needle)
- Clothes for customising
- Pencil or sewing chalk
- Needles, thread and scissors

Button it

You can brighten up a boring coat, cardie or dress by simply sewing on new buttons. Try a bright contrasting colour, giant buttons, or buttons that are all different.

Button and bead art

1 Decorate a top, jacket or hat with beads or buttons in a pattern. Start by sketching your design on paper.

2 Copy the design lightly onto the garment using a pencil or sewing chalk. Then sew the beads or buttons on to create your design.

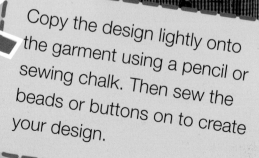

On the edge

1

Beads look great in a line around a collar or the edge of a pocket. To do this, thread a thin needle with some strong thread and knot the end.

2

Thread beads onto the needle and the thread, pushing them together. When you have enough, knot the other end too.

knot

3

Lay the string of beads where you want it, and carefully sew it in place all the way along, using overstitch (see page 9).

Funky footwear

Bored with your trainers? Change them! Canvas shoes are easy to re-colour using fabric paint – as long as they're a light colour to start with. You can add other decorations too.

Get the gear!

- Canvas shoes, with laces removed
- Fabric paint
- Cheap art paintbrush
- Newspaper, kitchen roll and rubber gloves
- For decorating, beads, buttons, ribbons, etc. and sewing equipment

1 It's best to paint shoes on the floor or even outdoors, away from carpets and sofas. Spread out the newspaper and wear rubber gloves.

2 Remove the laces before you start painting. Follow the fabric paint instructions and use the brush or applicator provided, or if there isn't one, a small art paintbrush. Put one hand inside the shoe and use the other hand to paint with.

3

You could paint spots, flowers, stripes or an all-over colour. Go slowly to avoid drips and smudges. If you are only painting part of the shoe, do the edges very carefully.

Tip!
Use a strong needle and extra-strong thread to sew through canvas, and check first that they can fit through your beads and buttons.

4

For extra decoration, or to jazz up darker shoes, use the methods from earlier in the book to sew on beads, buttons or ready-made fabric flowers.

Glam sandals

Take a simple pair of flip-flops, slide-on sandals or ballet pumps, and make them glamorous, pretty or super-sparkly.

Get the gear!

- Flip-flops, sandals or ballet pumps
- Shiny buttons, beads, fabric flowers or ribbons
- Scissors, sturdy needle and extra-strong thread
- **Thimble**

Stunning sandals

Sandals look great completely covered with beads or buttons. Sew them on one at a time, knotting the thread on the inside of the sandal.

Quick and easy

For a quicker project, sew a row of beads or buttons along an edge, or simply decorate each shoe with a fabric or felt flower (see page 10–11).

Tip!

Whether your sandals are leather, fabric, rubber or plastic, sewing them can be hard work. First use a needle to make the holes, then sew through them. If it's difficult to push the needle through, wear a thimble on your finger.

Ankle ties

1 Add ribbons to sandals to make ankle ties. For each sandal, cut two pieces of ribbon about 60cm long.

2 Sew the ends to the insides of your sandal straps, close to the ankle.

3 To wear, wrap the ribbons around your ankles (or further up the leg if you prefer) and tie in a bow.

Bow ties

For a simpler ribbon effect, just cut a length of ribbon and wrap or tie in a bow around your sandal or flip-flop straps.

Appliqué shapes

Appliqué means making a fabric picture, which you then 'apply' or sew onto something. Create any shape you like, and use it to decorate a T-shirt, hat, bag, cardie or jeans.

Get the gear!

- Paper, pencil and tape measure or ruler
- Scraps of flat, non-stretchy fabric, such as felt, **cord** or printed cotton
- Scissors, pins, needles and thread
- Sewing chalk

1 Start by sketching a shape on paper until you are happy with your design. A good size is about 6–12cm across.

2 Copy your shape onto your chosen fabric in pencil or sewing chalk. Here are a few shape ideas:

Tip!
Try cutting a ready-printed shape out of a fabric that has flowers or other interesting pictures on it.

3 Sew around the shape using backstitch (see page 7), just inside the edge of the shape. If you can use a sewing machine, you can do this on the machine by using a zigzag stitch (turn to the zigzag setting).

4 Carefully cut the shape out, leaving about 0.5cm around the stitching.

5 Pin the shape onto your garment and sew it in place, using overstitch (see page 9) around the edge, plus some backstitch across the middle. You could sew in a swirly or zigzag pattern, or use this stitching to add details. This will hold the shape in place firmly.

Appliqué advanced!

Once you've tried simple appliqué, you can piece together several bits of fabric to make a more complex design. Add beads and buttons to make eyes or other parts of the picture.

Get the gear!

- Paper and pencil
- Scraps of flat, non-stretchy fabric, such as felt, cord or printed cotton
- Scissors, pins, needles and thread

1

As before, design your appliqué first. Decide which fabrics to use for which parts, and how many pieces you will need. You may want to join pieces together side by side, like this...

or layer pieces on top of each other like this.

2

Following the method for appliqué on pages 26 and 27, mark your shapes on the fabric, sew around them, then cut them out.

Pin and sew them together using backstitch (see page 7), before attaching them to your garment.

3

Lastly, add any buttons or beads on top.

4

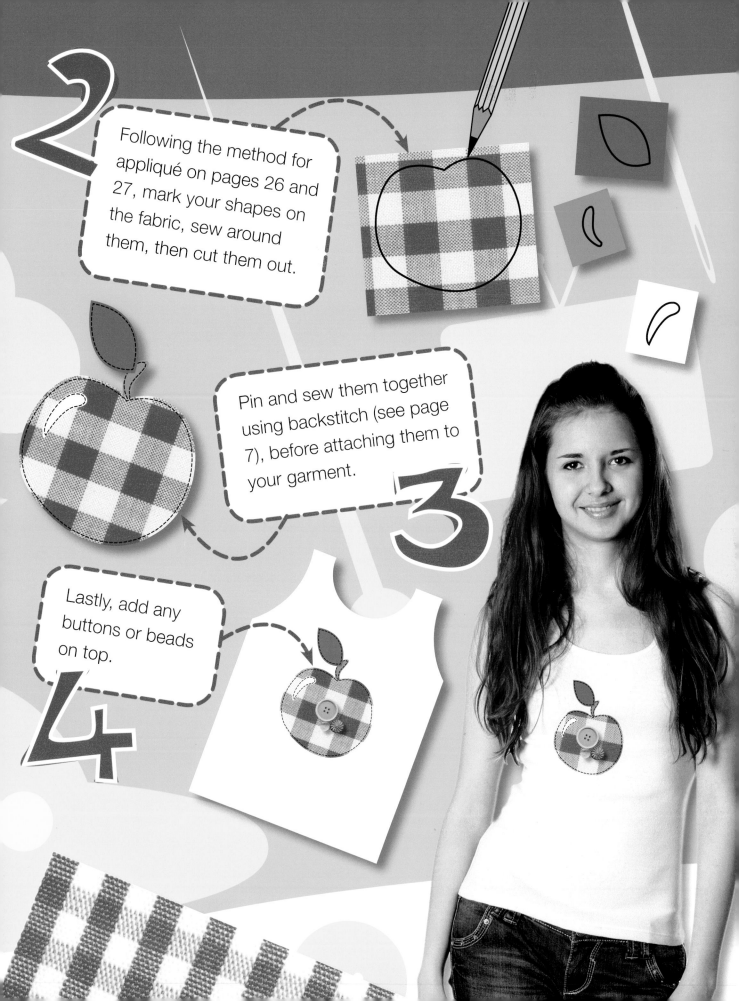

Equipment tips

Here's a quick guide to finding and using the gear you need for clothes-customising.

Beads
Craft shops, toy shops and sewing shops often have beads, and there are also specialist bead shops. You can reuse beads from old or broken jewellery too.

Buttons
You can buy buttons in sewing shops, craft shops and department stores. Also try charity shops and reusing buttons from old clothes.

Embroidery thread
This is often sold in sewing and craft shops or knitting shops, and comes in hundreds of colours. Look for good quality, cotton thread, such as Anchor, which is easy to use and washable.

Fabric
Fabric shops, craft shops and some department stores sell new fabrics by the metre. Check bargain buckets for cheaper **remnants**. IKEA® is great for cheap, funky fabric. Ask friends and family if they have old clothes, bed linen or curtains you could cut up and reuse.

Fabric paint
Craft shops, art shops and toy shops may have this.

Felt
Fabric shops, department stores, craft shops and toy shops often have felt.

Needles
From sewing shops. Look for a variety pack with lots of different sizes.

Old clothes
As well as reusing your own old fabrics, ask family members for anything they don't want any more, and check out charity shops and jumble sales.

Online
There are many fabric and craft shops on the Internet. You may find the following sites useful starting points:
www.handyhippo.co.uk
www.hobbycraft.co.uk
www.myfabrics.co.uk

Pins
From sewing shops. Longer pins with ball-shaped heads are the easiest to use.

Ready-made fabric flowers
From craft and sewing shops.

Ribbons
Sewing and fabric shops usually sell ribbons and trimmings by the metre.

Scissors
The sharper your scissors, the easier they are to work with, but take care when using them. Special sewing, craft or embroidery scissors from a sewing shop are best.

Sequins
You can often find these at craft shops and stationer's.

Sewing machines
This book doesn't show you how to use a sewing machine, but if you have one, you can use it for most of the projects. Follow the machine's instructions, and get an adult to help you. If you want to buy a sewing machine, try a department store or sewing shop.

Tape measure
From sewing, stationery or DIY shops.

Thread
From sewing shops. It's worth buying good quality thread as it's easier to sew with. Use extra-strong thread for sewing through heavy fabrics or shoes.

Glossary

appliqué
A technique used to decorate clothing or other fabric items by attaching fabric shapes.

backstitch
A strong sewing stitch that goes over each part of the fabric twice.

cord (short for corduroy)
A fabric with narrow ridges running along it.

corsage
A small bouquet of flowers worn on your clothes.

customise
To change something to suit you, or add your own designs.

embroidery
Using coloured thread to decorate fabric.

garment
An item of clothing.

gather
To pull fabric together into a bundle or crinkle using a line of stitching.

haberdashery
Ribbons, buttons, pins, needles and other sewing bits and bobs.

hem
The edge of a piece of fabric, folded over and sewn in place to stop it unravelling.

overstitch
A looping sewing stitch for sewing around edges.

remnants
Leftover pieces of fabric.

running stitch
A simple, in-and-out sewing stitch.

sequins
Little shiny or metallic discs with a hole in the middle.

sewing chalk
Sometimes called dressmaker's or tailor's chalk. Special chalk for marking fabric, available from sewing shops.

slogan
A word or phrase.

stash
A place where something is stored – such as your collection of fabrics and sewing stuff!

thimble
A hard cover that you put on your fingertip to help you push a needle through fabric.

Index